# POWER of PATTERNS

# CODING

**Rane Anderson**

## Consultants

**Timothy Rasinski, Ph.D.**
Kent State University

**Lori Oczkus, M.A.**
Literacy Consultant

**Publishing Credits**

Rachelle Cracchiolo, M.S.Ed., *Publisher*

Conni Medina, M.A.Ed., *Managing Editor*

Dona Herweck Rice, *Series Developer*

Emily R. Smith, M.A.Ed., *Content Director*

Stephanie Bernard/Noelle Cristea, M.A.Ed., *Editors*

Robin Erickson, *Senior Graphic Designer*

The TIME logo is a registered trademark of TIME Inc. Used under license.

**Image Credits:** p.4 Scott Olson/iStockphoto.com; pp.4–5 NG Images/Alamy Stock Photo; pp.6–7 hocus-focus/iStockphoto.com; p.18 Hans Hillewaert, used under Creative Commons BY-SA 4.0; pp.19, 20–21, 22–23, 25, 28–29, 33, 35, 36–37, 40 Scratch is a project of the Lifelong Kindergarten group at the MIT Media Lab. See http://scratch.mit.edu; all other images from iStock and/or Shutterstock.

**Note:** The answers to the mathematical problems posed throughout the book are provided on page 48.

**Library of Congress Cataloging-in-Publication Data**

Names: Anderson, Rane, author.
Title: Power of patterns : coding / Rane Anderson.
Other titles: Coding
Description: Huntington Beach, CA : Teacher Created Materials, [2017] | Audience: Grades 7 to 8. | Includes index.
Identifiers: LCCN 2016047694 (print) | LCCN 2016056196 (ebook) | ISBN 9781493836253 (pbk.) | ISBN 9781480757295 (eBook)
Subjects: LCSH: Computer programming–Juvenile literature.
Classification: LCC QA76.6 .A4697 2017 (print) | LCC QA76.6 (ebook) | DDC 005.1–dc23
LC record available at https://lccn.loc.gov/2016047694

**Teacher Created Materials**
5301 Oceanus Drive
Huntington Beach, CA 92649-1030
http://www.tcmpub.com

**ISBN 978-1-4938-3625-3**

# Table of Contents

# A Coder's Dream

Imagine creating a useful tool that will make life better for thousands of people simply by your writing words on a page. With **computer programming**, you don't have to imagine it; you can make it happen.

Computer programming helps turn dreams into reality. Someone once dreamed of sharing thoughts, photos, and messages with people around the world. And now, people can do that through social media. Gamers once dreamed of adventuring through uncharted territory. So computer programmers, often called coders, developed virtual worlds. Employees at NASA once dreamed of exploring the surface of Mars. They programmed robots that can travel there and collect environmental data. Each of these **innovations** depended on computer programming to bring it to life. From social media to artificial intelligence, **coding** can make our wildest dreams come true. The only limit is our imaginations.

## Computer Science for All

In President Barack Obama's 2016 State of the Union Address, he announced his plan to bring computer science into all schools in the Unites States. He said that students of all grade levels should learn the skills to create digital technologies. He considers computer science, including coding, a basic skill.

## That's *So* Coded

Most electronic objects people use on a daily basis require coding. Video game consoles, cell phones, tablets, pacemakers, alarm clocks, and so many other items rely on coding.

the *Curiosity* Mars rover

# Coding Basics

Many people spend several hours each week in front of computer screens, tablets, or mobile devices. Screen time provides entertainment, keeps us connected with family and friends, and is a great outlet for learning about virtually anything. All of this screen time takes place on just the "surface" of computer coding, in what's called the **graphical user interface** (GUI). GUI is often pronounced like the word *gooey* by those in the coding world.

But hidden behind the GUI is a complex world of words and symbols that build the apps, software, and websites people love. These words, or lines of code, bring computers and other electronics to life. Coding helps to create all kinds of **programs**, from role-playing games to the programs used by medical devices that might one day save your life.

## Medical Devices

Devices such as heart rate monitors, sleep sensors, and blood pressure machines run on computer programs. Other programmed devices take more active roles in maintaining the health of patients. For example, insulin pumps and other drug-delivery devices get the right amounts of medicine to patients right when they need it most.

## Matched!

If someone wants to donate a kidney to a family member but is not a good match, there's a computer program that can help. This program keeps track of potential donors and searches for other viable matches. In a paired-exchange donation, when a match is found, the donor can give a kidney to that person and hopefully earn a viable kidney for his or her family member in return.

## Computer Recipes

If you wanted to bake cookies, how would you begin? You might start by gathering all the necessary ingredients, such as flour, butter, sugar, eggs, and chocolate chips. But you would also need the recipe to tell you how to bake everything once it's combined. After all, the ingredients can't bake themselves. That's exactly how computers and other electronic devices work. Electronic devices possess all the ingredients needed to perform impressive tasks. But by itself, an electronic device cannot accomplish much besides basic arithmetic. Electronic devices need very specific instructions, like a recipe, to complete complex operations. That's why coders write **source code**.

## The Source Code Story

Computer magic begins with a coder dreaming up an idea. But to get that idea to actually work on a computer or another electronic device, the coder must first write the source code. The source code contains the step-by-step instructions written in words, numbers, and symbols that will make a program run.

# PEMDAS

When we start to evaluate an expression, we must follow a specific order. This is known as the order of operations. You might have heard the saying "Please Excuse My Dear Aunt Sally."

| Please | Parentheses |
|--------|-------------|
| Excuse | Exponents |
| My Dear | Multiply/Divide (left to right) |
| Aunt Sally | Add/Subtract (left to right) |

To correctly solve an expression, follow the precise instructions of the order of operations. Don't ignore the *left to right* requirements because, if you do, you'll get the wrong answer. A computer program also relies on precise instructions that follow a specific order.

## PEMDAS in Action

$$\frac{(18 + 2 \cdot 3)}{2^2}$$

Evaluate this expression in whatever order you see fit, completely ignoring the PEMDAS rule. Try it again using a different order. Lastly, solve it using the order of operations, and check your answer on page 48. This should illustrate that very different answers will result based on the order in which you solve. But what matters most in this problem is finding the correct answer. What do you think would happen if the source code of a program were written out of order?

# Route Algorithms

Type in an address on a map or GPS **application**, and it will search for the shortest, fastest route available. But how exactly does the application find the best route? Computer programmers use **algorithms** to solve problems like this and include them in the source code of programs.

## Algorithm for Area

You have probably encountered an algorithm in your math class. For example, the steps to calculate the area of a circle are an algorithm:

1. Measure the radius of the circle.
2. Square the radius (multiply the radius by itself).
3. Multiply the result by π (3.14).

$$A = π × r^2$$

If the radius of a circle is the distance from its center to the edge and the diameter is 2r, what is the area of a circle with a diameter of 4 feet?

# An aMAZEing Escape!

Imagine that you need to discover the quickest route off your school campus. Create an algorithm that helps find the fastest way out of the school maze. Search for possible routes while also determining the best route for immediate escape. Then, generate your route algorithm by writing instructions using directional words like *right*, *left*, *up*, and *down*. Also include the number of blocks to travel per move. Format your instructions in the following style:

```
Walk [direction] [#] space/s
```

# Coding Languages

Hello! こんにちは! Bonjour! Habari! Ciao! !שלום

Similar to people, computers "speak" many different languages. In the early days of coding, computer programmers used **machine code** to write computer commands. This difficult language consists of dizzying strings of 0s and 1s called *binary numbers*. It's challenging for people to read and write machine code. That's partly why hardly anyone uses it today. But it remains the only language a computer's processor can read entirely without the assistance of another program. In fact, all programs must be translated into machine code to run.

High-level languages account for a large percentage of the languages used to write programs. These languages use dictionary words and **syntax** that are more easily read by humans. So not only is it easy for people to read and write, but it's also much simpler for coders to express complex ideas within the source code. That opens a world of possibilities.

## C++

C++ is a relatively old language, but it is a workhorse in the programming world. It excels at creating robust, precise, and high-performance programs. It is the language of choice for video games and financial and manufacturing systems.

## Spot the Code

Practice distinguishing between machine code and different high-level languages. Can you spot the differences?

```
resultSet = db.executeQuery(select *
    from users where Fname='john');

0001010110101110101010100100100101

String lastName = resultSet.
    getString("Lname");

00000101110101010110001101011001
```

### Python®

Python is a general-purpose, high-level programming language. It has very simple syntax, which makes it easy to program. It is also *open source*, which means a user can download the **compiler** and tools for free. Python can be used to write application software and to script the sequence of instructions needed for a web application.

# Source Code Translators

People can travel from one side of the world to the other in under a day. Often this means travelers are suddenly immersed in a country where potentially nobody else speaks their native language. How might a traveler order dinner at a restaurant in a foreign country? How would he or she locate a hotel? Many people use **translators** to convert words from one language into another. The technology company Waverly Labs has designed an earpiece system called Pilot®. Two people who speak different languages each wear an earpiece. Using a speech recognition app, the earpiece translates the dialogue directly into the users' ears.

Computers also rely on translators to convert the source code of high-level languages into machine code. In computer programming, there are two types of translators: compilers and interpreters. Simply put, a compiler translates an entire program and *then* executes it. An interpreter translates each line of code and executes them one by one.

Have you ever noticed a computer file that ends in the extension .exe? This file contains the machine code of a program that has been compiled from source code. Compiled files only run on the type of computer they were designed for. For example, you can't run an .exe file on a Macintosh operating system because .exe programs were designed to run on Windows machines.

Interpreters translate source code into machine code as the program runs. Interpreted code runs on many types of operating systems. A versatile language such as Java® is compatible with thousands of devices from computers and phones to coffee makers and cars.

## Java

Java is an interpreted language, which means that Java code can run on any device supporting Java. According to Java's publisher, Oracle®, over five billion devices run the language platform. Java has similar syntax and capabilities to C++, but it runs much slower because it is an interpreted language and only runs one line of code at a time.

# The Pre-code Code

If you have to write an essay, a book report, or a research paper, what's your prewriting strategy? Most writers begin the writing process by brainstorming and outlining their ideas. Many beginning coders follow this same process.

Writing source code in a high-level language takes a lot of time and patience. So coders often begin brainstorming or detailing their ideas for programs using a fake language called *pseudocode*. Pseudocode is a simplified version of high-level language that's used for program planning rather than execution. Think of it as a rough draft. It allows a new coder to translate an idea into code without focusing too much time or energy on writing perfect source code. Take a look at this pseudocode for a hypothetical quiz program:

```
Ask User "Who famously said 'I'm
    the president of the United
    States and I'm not going to
    eat any more broccoli'?"
option "A) Barack Obama"
option "B) Jimmy Carter"
option "C) George H. W. Bush"
option "D) Teddy Roosevelt"
Get user's answer
If the answer is C, Then
    output "You got it right!!"
```

### Scratch®

Some coders use **visual programming languages**. In a visual programming language, coders can manipulate elements of the program graphically. In Scratch, one of many visual programming languages, users can create games, tell animated stories, and design simulations using code blocks and pictures.

Score  0

What is 7 x 9?

### Here's an Idea!

Some users—including teachers—use Scratch to explain mathematical concepts. Using Scratch to illustrate math will sometimes make a challenging concept easier to understand. Scratch users can also create their own games to help practice certain math skills.

Every written language, including English, comes with a set of rules to follow. In school, students learn to capitalize the first word of every sentence. We also learn to complete each sentence with punctuation such as a period, an exclamation point, or a question mark. Students also learn that sentences require a subject and a predicate.

Just as the language rules for Japanese and English are different, each programming language also has its own unique syntax. And if the rules of whichever programming language being used are not followed, the program will either do something you don't want it to do, or it may not run at all. Learning to use a programming language can be as difficult as learning a foreign language. Both take a considerable amount of time and practice to achieve fluency.

## Rosetta Stone

The discovery of the Rosetta Stone in 1799 allowed scholars to translate Egyptian hieroglyphs. A decree by King Ptolemy V of Egypt was chiseled into the same stone three times: once in hieroglyphs, once in Egyptian **demotic** script, and once in ancient Greek. By comparing the three versions, two of which the scholars could understand, they were able to finally translate Egyptian hieroglyphs.

These four languages may look different, but they all have the same output.

| | |
|---|---|
| Java | ```java
for (int index = 1; index <= 5; index++)
{
        System.out.print(index + " ");
}
System.out.println();
``` |
| Python | ```python
for index in range(1, 6):
    print index," "
``` |
| VisualBasic | ```vb
For index As Integer = 1 To 5
    Debug.Write(index.ToString & " ")
Next
Debug.WriteLine("")
``` |
| Scratch | |
| Output for all: | 1 2 3 4 5 |

# STOP! THINK...

○ What differences do you notice among the various source code examples?

○ What are some similarities between the different source code examples?

○ Which of these languages do you think would be easiest to learn, and why?
```

# Basics in Scratch

New coders often use Scratch as a learning tool and as a gateway to the more difficult high-level languages. Scratch uses color-coded "blocks" of code—rather than plain text—to create instructions. Using the blocks, coders can design all sorts of programs. Some examples include interactive tools for learning, games, animations, and art. Unlike textual coding languages, visual programming languages allow coders to drag and drop premade sections of code. This allows coders to build programs as if they were building with toy blocks. In this way, the different shapes and colors visually show the necessary syntax.

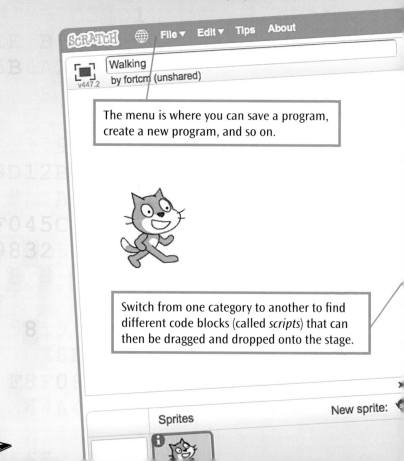

The menu is where you can save a program, create a new program, and so on.

Switch from one category to another to find different code blocks (called *scripts*) that can then be dragged and dropped onto the stage.

# The Scratch GUI

Codes can program **sprites** to accomplish many different types of things, such as walking, dancing, talking, or embarking on an adventure.

Click this tab to add sounds to accompany different parts of your program.

Drag and drop blocks of code on the stage to arrange instructions for your program.

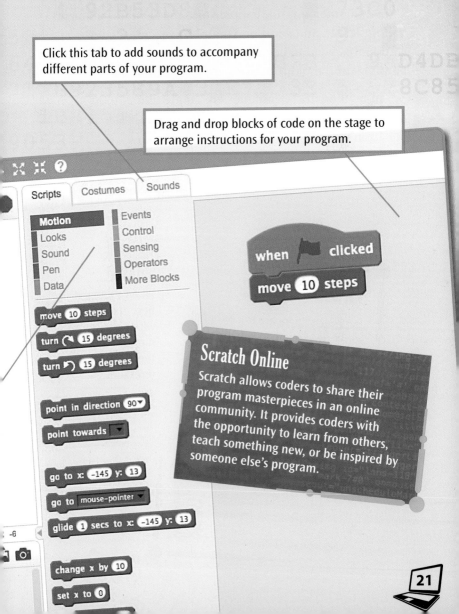

Scripts    Costumes    Sounds

Motion
Looks
Sound
Pen
Data

Events
Control
Sensing
Operators
More Blocks

when ▶ clicked
move 10 steps

move 10 steps
turn ↻ 15 degrees
turn ↺ 15 degrees

point in direction 90▾
point towards ▾

go to x: -145 y: 13
go to mouse-pointer ▾
glide 1 secs to x: -145 y: 13

change x by 10
set x to 0

## Scratch Online
Scratch allows coders to share their program masterpieces in an online community. It provides coders with the opportunity to learn from others, teach something new, or be inspired by someone else's program.

-6

# Variables

Have you ever programmed your favorite station into a car radio? If you have, then you have already used one very basic component of coding called a *variable*. A variable stores a value, such as a number or word, which represents something meaningful. People store these values and can manipulate them later. For example, you can set a pop station this year and change it to a rap station next year. The numbers of the radio stations are stored in variables.

In mathematics, variables are single letters used to represent unknown values. What are the variables in the equation below?

$$y = 8x - 21$$

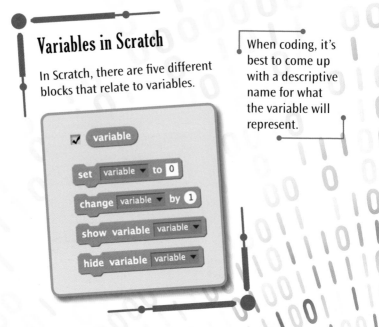

## Variables in Scratch

In Scratch, there are five different blocks that relate to variables.

When coding, it's best to come up with a descriptive name for what the variable will represent.

☑ variable

set variable ▼ to 0

change variable ▼ by 1

show variable variable ▼

hide variable variable ▼

In many video games, a health bar tracks a player's health. Obstacles or events may occur in the game that either injure or restore the player's health. Below is what a health bar might look like for a hypothetical game written in Scratch. In this game, touching lightning will hurt a player's health. In order for the computer to be able to remember this value and keep track of how it changes, it's stored in the variable.

## Input and Output

Think about your favorite computer games, video games, or board games. Now, imagine that suddenly you cannot play them anymore and you're only allowed to watch. How boring is that?

In coding, *input* is a user interacting with a program, and *output* is what happens as a result of the input. Think of input and output as having a cause-and-effect relationship. Different languages have very different ways of getting input into programs. In one program, an interaction could be the click of a button or the typing of a word into a pop-up. By making a program interactive, you can complete more interesting tasks.

## Input and Output with GUIs

In the old days, computers had text-based interfaces where users could only read plain text on a screen and type text commands on the keyboard. But now, with GUIs, a user can click, tap, and drag buttons or images on the screen to tell the program to do something—this provides tons of great input and output.

### Garbage In, Garbage Out Principle

If a program prompts "enter a number between 1 and 10" and "hello" is entered instead, it will likely give a meaningless result. Or it might stop working all together. **Input validation** helps avoid this problem.

# Input and Output in Scratch

Scratch's GUI makes it easy to set up input and output. The following code will ask for the user's name, greet the user, and then perform a calculation to find out how many letters are in the user's name.

```
when [flag] clicked
ask  What is your name?  and wait
say  join  join  Hello,  answer   !   for 2 secs
say  join  join  Your name has   length of  answer    letters in it.  for 10 secs
```

What is your name?

# Boolean Expressions

Imagine that you get an allowance every Friday at 6 p.m. To get that allowance, you must first meet certain conditions ahead of time, such as completing all homework and chores. As 6 p.m. on Friday rolls around, your parents will verify whether the responsibilities have been completed. There are only two options: yes or no.

In computer programming, a Boolean expression establishes whether something is true or false. And the answer to the question helps the computer decide how to proceed. In the allowance example, a *true* or *false* question will indicate how to proceed: Should your parents award the allowance or not? In other words, a Boolean expression is like a test that requires two values to compare and an **operator** to define the test.

## Comparing Values

This is what a Boolean expression looks like using a mathematical test:

$$x < 5$$

This compares two values, $x$ and 5.

Assuming that $x$ represents an unknown integer, this statement will determine if the value of $x$ is 4 or lower. If it is, this statement will evaluate to true. Otherwise, it will evaluate to false.

$$x > 5$$

This statement will determine if the value of $x$ is 6 or higher.

$$x == 5$$

This statement will determine if the value of $x$ is exactly 5.

### The Double Equal Sign

Notice that the last example uses a double equal sign. In most programming languages, a single equal sign ($x = 5$) stores the value of 5 into the variable $x$. A double equal sign will test to see if two values are equal.

### True or False?

If $x$ is less than 4 but greater than 1, is the following equation true or false?

$$7\,(x + 2) \geq 42$$

Conditional Booleans determine if a certain condition, or circumstance, has occurred. The bright blue "touching edge" Boolean block (the hexagonal shape indicates it is a Boolean block) tests to see if the car has reached the edge of the stage. If it has reached the edge of the stage, the program will then turn the car around.

Comparative Booleans compare the values of two different numbers. Usually, they compare the value of a variable to a static value, a value that doesn't change.

**What color is the sky?**

Type answer here.

```
when ⚑ clicked
ask What color is the sky? and wait
if     answer = blue   then
    play sound cheer ▾ until done
    say You got it! for 2 secs
else
    play sound duck ▾ until done
    say Try again! for 2 secs
```

The green Boolean block tests to see if the value within the variable "answer" is equal to "blue."

## Conditional Boolean Blocks in Scratch

`key space ▾ pressed?` This block tests if the user is pressing a certain key on the keyboard.

`mouse down?` This block tests if the user has pressed down on the mouse button.

`touching ▾ ?` This block tests if the sprite is touching the object selected in the drop down box.

`touching color ■ ?` This block tests if the sprite is touching any object of the color shown.

# Conditional Statements

You probably use conditional statements every day without even realizing it.

- *"If* the weather is nice, *then* I'll go to the beach today."
- *"If* I win the tickets, *then* I'll take a friend to the concert."
- *"If* I get an A on this exam, *then* I'll get an A in the class."

In coding, a conditional statement, also called an **if-then statement**, instructs a program that *if x* is true, *then y* should happen next. If this sounds similar to Boolean expressions, that's because it is. Boolean expressions play a large role in conditional statements.

Think back to the example about getting an allowance. *If* the right conditions were met (i.e., homework and chores are complete Friday before 6 p.m.), *then* your parents give you the allowance money. Actually, giving the money would be what your parents—or "the computer"—decide to accomplish next. In other words, *if* something is true, the computer will be instructed to *then* run a specific block of code.

# BASIC Code Fun

Imagine you are writing a quiz program. First, you would write code to ask the user a question. You would also write code to provide the user with four possible answers. Then, you would want to check to see if the correct answer is entered. Here is the BASIC code for this scenario. See if you can get it right. This code shows the user selected "C":

```
print "A TV advertisement claims that
    5 out of 6 dentists recommend Acme
    toothpaste. If 900 dentists were
    surveyed, how many recommended Acme
    toothpaste?"
print "A) 750"
print "B) 1,080"
print "C) 300"
print "D) 600"
answer = prompt("What is your answer?")
If (answer == C) Then
    print "Your answer is C."
End If
```

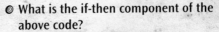

**THINK LINK**

- What is the if-then component of the above code?
- Do the math to determine if the correct answer is C.
- What might happen if the user gets the answer wrong?

# The If-Then-Else Statement

An if-then-else statement builds on an if-then statement. An else statement is used to do something *if* the condition in the if-then statement ends up being false. We use these statements in everyday situations.

- "*If* the weather is nice, *then* I'll go to the beach today, or *else* I will go swimming at the gym's indoor pool."

- "*If* I win the tickets, *then* I'll take a friend to the concert, or *else* I will split the cost of the extra ticket."

In the quiz program example on the previous page, the user selected C as the answer, which is, in fact, incorrect. To better explain why, here's a breakdown of the statement:

Of the dentists surveyed, 5 out of 6, or about 83 percent, recommend Acme toothpaste. So, to solve this word problem, we multiply 0.83 by 900.

$$(0.83) \times (900) = 750 \text{ dentists}$$

Therefore, the correct answer is A.

When writing a quiz program, it is essential to account for the user's correct answers as well as incorrect answers. To do this, the if-then statement can be rewritten like this:

```
If( answer == A ) Then
    print "Your answer is right."
Else
    print "Your answer is wrong.
    The correct answer is A."
End If
```

## Problems with *Then*

Sometimes, coders fail to tell the program where the if-then statement ends. But in programs such as Scratch, it's easy to visually identify where it should end. For instance, the orange if-then code block wraps its "arms" around the section of code that will run if the statement is true.

What color is the sky?

Type answer here.

```
when 🏁 clicked

ask  What color is the sky?  and wait

if       answer  =  blue   then

    play sound  cheer ▾  until done

    say  You got it!  for 2 secs

else

    play sound  duck ▾  until done

    say  Try again!  for 2 secs
```

# Loops

Computers complete repetitive tasks quickly and efficiently. To make this happen, coders break down the tasks they want to accomplish into sets of repetitive steps that can leverage the computer's power. When making a peanut butter sandwich, one step is "spread the peanut butter." But this single part of the process can be broken down into many substeps:

a. Insert knife into peanut butter jar.

b. Scoop up peanut butter.

c. Remove knife from jar.

d. Spread peanut butter onto bread.

To people, it's obvious to only spread enough peanut butter to cover the bread. But computers need extremely specific instructions. A computer would need to know exactly when to start and stop spreading the peanut butter. If a computer is just told, "spread peanut butter onto bread," it will go into an **infinite loop**. It doesn't know when to stop or even if it *should* ever stop.

Infinite loops could be problematic if the task a computer is told to do isn't meant to repeat forever. The computer will get stuck in the loop and never move on to the next task. So coders need to indicate an *exit condition*, otherwise the loop will remain stuck infinitely repeating the same step.

## Loops in Scratch

Scratch clearly identifies different types of loops. For example, one loop may be labeled "forever" while another may be labeled "repeat 10." A hexagonal shape will indicate a Boolean test block that will repeat until the Boolean becomes true.

forever

repeat 10

repeat until

# Do-While Loop

In a do-while loop, the computer performs each step of the instructions only once, and when it reaches the end of the instructions, the computer checks the exit condition. If the exit condition is true, the computer repeats the steps. Upon reaching the end of the steps, it once again checks the exit condition. If the exit condition is *still* true, it repeats the process again. However, as soon as the exit condition is false, the program exits the loop and proceeds to the next statement.

## Do-While Loop in Pseudocode

Do {

   a.  Insert knife into peanut butter jar

   b.  Scoop up peanut butter

   c.  Remove knife from jar

   d.  Spread peanut butter onto a slice of bread

} While (Bread is less than completely covered)

In the example above, an exit condition has been added to the end of the instructions. In doing so, spreading peanut butter is now a do-while loop. In the example below, the lack of an exit condition means the car will keep driving back and forth forever.

infinite loop example

```
when [flag] clicked
go to x: -140 y: -70
forever
    move 10 steps
    wait 0.05 secs
    if < touching edge ▼ ? > then
        turn ↻ 180 degrees
```

# Loops in Scratch

Let's take a look at the code used to create loops in Scratch. In this example, the "forever" loop was replaced with the "repeat until" loop. This means that now the car will continuously move only until it touches the edge of the stage, and then it will exit the loop. Then, the following commands will make the car turn and drive up the street a little just before the program ends.

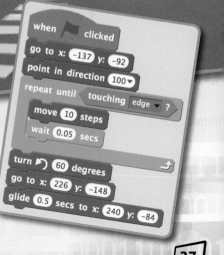

"repeat until" loop example

when 🏳 clicked
go to x: -137 y: -92
point in direction 100▼
repeat until   touching edge ▼ ?
    move 10 steps
    wait 0.05 secs
turn ↻ 60 degrees
go to x: 226 y: -148
glide 0.5 secs to x: 240 y: -84

# Debugging

When you finish coding your very first program, you'll undoubtedly expect to see the miraculous results of all the time and effort devoted to the task. So you sit back and expect to watch your masterpiece at work. But then . . . nothing happens. Or maybe something does happen, but it goes very, very wrong.

This is a familiar story that many coders, professionals included, could tell, and it's the reason **debugging** is such an important element of computer programming. Coders will sometimes spend hours trying to determine why programs don't run or why there are strange glitches that are not supposed to exist. **Troubleshooting** what the problem is and then how to debug it requires patience and perseverance.

### Find the Error

Locating the error within code requires the same critical-thinking skills needed to find an error in a math problem. Take a moment to practice those skills here. The answer to the following problem is incorrect. Try to locate the error.

$$(3a^2 + 6a - 2) + (2a^2 - 8a - 7)$$
$$3a^2 + 6a - 2 + 2a^2 - 8a - 7$$
$$5a^2 + 6a - 2 - 8a - 7$$
$$= 5a^2 - 2a - 5$$

## The General Idea

Unfortunately, there's no foolproof, step-by-step method to debug a program. The process of debugging can be lengthy and often includes a lot of trial and error. To begin debugging, consider the following questions:

- Are the commands logical?
- Are important commands missing within the code?
- Are any commands out of order?
- Are there commands inside an if-then statement that should be outside it or vice versa?

### Ask the Community

When all else fails—ask a friend. If the program you work with is shared with an online community, chances are many coders will come to the rescue. This shouldn't be the first step in the debugging process, however. Trust yourself, and put in the time and patience. It'll make you a better coder!

### Practice, Practice, Practice!

Scratchers post debugging activities online for you to practice your debugging skills. Do a search on the Scratch website for debugging activities, and you will find many. Also, just as you might ask the community to help debug your program, you can also practice your troubleshooting skills by helping other coders who ask for help.

# Troubleshooting the Code

In the program below, you must guess a number between 1 and 10. In turn, the sprite will declare whether your answer is too high or too low, but this part of the code doesn't work consistently. Review each line of the code to troubleshoot the problem.

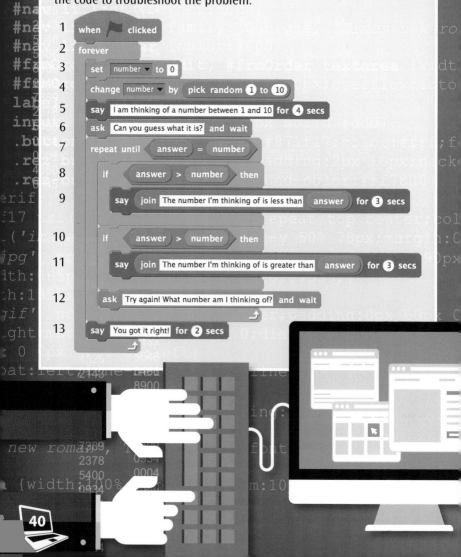

```
1   when [flag] clicked
2   forever
3     set number to 0
4     change number by (pick random 1 to 10)
5     say [I am thinking of a number between 1 and 10] for 4 secs
6     ask [Can you guess what it is?] and wait
7     repeat until < answer = number >
8       if < answer > number > then
9         say (join [The number I'm thinking of is less than] answer) for 3 secs
10        if < answer > number > then
11          say (join [The number I'm thinking of is greater than] answer) for 3 secs
12        ask [Try again! What number am I thinking of?] and wait
13    say [You got it right!] for 2 secs
```

# The Fix

- It's efficient to begin troubleshooting the part of the code that presents an obvious problem when the program runs. Since the problem concerns the *less than* or *greater than* function, the debugging process begins there.

- Line 8 checks if the user's answer is greater than the "random number" chosen by the program. If it's greater than the "random number," the program proceeds to line 9. Otherwise, it skips to line 10.

- Line 9 tells the user that he or she needs to guess a lower number.

- Line 10 checks to see if the user's answer is greater than the "random number," which is the same as line 8.

It looks as though two if-then statements check for the same condition. One needs to check for [answer < number] and the other needs to check [answer > number]. Therefore, Line 10 should be changed to "if answer < number then."

# Evolution of Code

Computers today accomplish millions of steps in the blink of an eye, and computer programmers have designed each one of those steps. Even doing something as simple as logging on to a website requires hundreds of concepts written by thousands of different programmers. Programmers have dreamed of and built remarkable tools to help the world become a better place. As a result of their hard work, people have been able to crack enemy ciphers during World War II, send rockets into space, and connect nearly every corner of the world to the Internet.

It's now up to the future generation of coders: you. You have the power to continue shaping the world through code. What great challenges can you think of? And how might a computer program solve those challenges? Always dream big, but remember that from humble beginnings come great things. This means that it's all right to start small. While you learn to code, try to imagine how you can make a difference at home or at school. Even small steps mean you're moving in the right direction.

## The Workplace Fun Zone

A huge number of companies try to attract talented computer programmers by making the workplace as interactive and fun as possible. Many software and Internet companies stock break rooms full of food and drinks, and provide game rooms for foosball or table tennis. Some even have areas for coders to take naps during breaks.

## A Wise Message

"Whether you want to uncover the secrets of the universe, or you want to pursue a career in the twenty-first century, basic computer programming is an essential skill to learn."

—Stephen Hawking, theoretical physicist, cosmologist, and author

# Glossary

**algorithms**—step-by-step procedures used to solve problems

**application**—a software program that helps users perform activities like word processing or video editing

**coding**—changing information into numbers, letters, or symbols

**compiler**—a program that translates the source code of a high-level language into executable machine code

**computer programming**—the process of writing computer software, which mostly consists of defining a problem, writing code to solve it, and then releasing computer programs

**debugging**—analyzing source code to locate typos, poor logic, or improper syntax that creates a glitch in the program

**demotic**—cursive form of Egyptian hieroglyphs

**graphical user interface**—the icons and visual indicators that allow a user to interact with an operating system or program

**if-then statement**—allows a program to do one thing if a Boolean expression evaluates to true, or nothing if the Boolean evaluates to false

**infinite loop**—a loop that does not have an exit condition and therefore continues to execute the same sequence of steps forever

**innovations**—new ideas, methods, or products that solve a problem

**input validation**—a series of logical checks performed when a user types something into a program to ensure that the input is the expected response

**machine code**—computer commands that a processor can understand directly; written only using binary numbers

**operator**—small function that performs common tasks, such as adding, subtracting, comparing, or storing values; often represented by only one or two symbols

**programs**—written sets of instructions for computers that will help them perform specific tasks

**source code**—instructions for a computer written in a human-readable, high-level language

**sprites**—objects in Scratch that perform the functions

**syntax**—the order of words in a phrase, clause, or sentence

**translators**—tools used to convert the words of one language into another language

**troubleshooting**—investigating what causes bugs or problems in programs or computers

**visual programming languages**—coding languages that allows the user to manipulate elements of a program graphically instead of textually

# Index

**PHP**

**jQuery**

**</CODE>**

**JS**

**Ruby**

**HTML&CSS**

**Python**

# Check It Out!

## Books

DK Publishing. 2014. *Help Your Kids with Computer Coding*. DK.

Marji, Majed. 2013. *Learn to Program with Scratch: A Visual Introduction to Programming with Games, Art, Science, and Math*. No Starch Press.

Sande, Warren, and Carter Sande. 2013. *Hello World! Computer Programming for Kids and Other Beginners*. Manning Publications.

Weyn, Suzanne. 2004. *The Bar Code Tattoo*. Scholastic.

———. 2012. *The Bar Code Prophecy*. Scholastic.

———. 2016. *The Bar Code Rebellion*. Scholastic.

## Video

Lifelong Kindergarten Group. *Getting Started with Scratch*. MIT Media Lab.

## Websites

Code.org®. *Learn an Hour of Code*. https://code.org/learn.

Lifelong Kindergarten Group. *Scratch*. https://scratch.mit .edu/.

Lifelong Kindergarten Group. *Scratch Wiki*. http://wiki .scratch.mit.edu/wiki/Scratch_Wiki_Home.

# Try It!

Coding is an integral part of our technological world and a skill that should be taught to all students. Write a letter to a leader explaining the benefits of coding education. Before writing your letter, you have some work to do:

- Decide on your speaking points. Why do you think coding in schools might benefit the next generation? Make a list of these points.

- Select three strong arguments to focus on in your letter. Support your arguments with research. Don't forget to include counterpoints and/or perspectives.

- Survey friends and/or kids in your school to see if they agree. Make sure you can use the information as support for your letter.

- Write a draft of your letter. Have two classmates edit and suggest additions or counterpoints to make your letter stronger. Rewrite a final draft using letter format.

- Research the address of the district, city council, and/or congressperson who funds education policy in your area. Mail your letter!

# About the Author

Rane Anderson lives in Colorado with her husband and son. She earned a bachelor of science in geology from California State University, Long Beach. When she's not writing or scaling mountains looking for cool geologic features, she's trying to program her toddler to take long naps, to never say no, and to eat his vegetables!

## Answers

page 9—PEMDAS in Action: Using the order of operations, the problem breaks down as follows:

$(18 + 2 \cdot 3)/2^2$

$(18 + 6)/2^2$

$24/2^2$

$24/4$

$= 6$

page 10—Dig Deeper: 12.56 square feet

page 27—True or False?: False. A true equation could be $7(x + 2) \leq 42$.

page 38—Find the Error: The error is in the last step. Since $-2 - 7 = -9$, the answer should come to $5a^2 - 2a - 9$.